THE DOLPHINS OF HILTON HEAD

THE DOLPHINS OF HILTON HEAD

Their Natural History

Cara M. Gubbins

University of South Carolina Press

Published in Columbia, South Carolina, by the
University of South Carolina Press

Manufactured in the United States of America

06 05 04 03 02   5 4 3 2 1

Library of Congress Cataloging-in-Publication Data

Gubbins, Cara M., 1964–
  The dolphins of Hilton Head : their natural history / Cara M. Gubbins.
  p. cm.
Includes bibliographical references (p. 69).
  ISBN 1-57003-458-3 (pbk. : alk. paper)
  1. Bottlenose dolphin—South Carolina—Hilton Head Island. I. Title.
    QL737.C432 G835 2002
    599.53'3'09757—dc21   2002003106

This book is dedicated to the dolphins of Hilton Head and all of the dolphins that I have worked with over the course of my life. My personal, scientific, and professional lives have been enriched greatly by the opportunity to share their worlds for a little while.

Every single species of the animal kingdom challenges us with all, or nearly all, of the mysteries of life.

Karl von Frisch,
honeybee researcher and Nobel Prize laureate

CONTENTS

ILLUSTRATIONS

PREFACE

One does not meet oneself until one catches the reflection in an eye
other than human.

Loren Eisley, scientist and author

Dolphins have always fascinated us. Centuries ago, someone must have looked
into the eye of a dolphin and seen herself there, beginning the endless attraction
between our two species. This glimpse of oneself in a dolphin's eye probably
occurs daily somewhere in the world. Firmly rooted in our collective consciousness, appearing in our myths, art, and literature for millennia, dolphins seem to
embody all the traits that we have and those to which we aspire. Their graceful
form and joyful athleticism win our hearts, and the attraction remains.

What is it that attracts humans to dolphins and other animals? E. O. Wilson,
the Harvard University sociobiologist and author, believes that there is a genetic
basis for our love of animals, something embedded in the very cells of our bodies
that drives us to touch and interact with wild and domesticated animals. He calls
this inherent tendency to focus on and affiliate with other life forms "biophilia."
According to Wilson, our relationships with animals form a fundamental part of
our existence.

*Dolphins have fascinated humans for centuries. Hilton Head dolphins seem to be
curious about us, too.*

   Modern people have a strong need to establish some kind of personal contact with wild animals, perhaps to end the "long loneliness" that the anthropologist and author Loren Eisley believes is the legacy of our evolution from our animal roots. Maybe we want to reach out and touch some primitive part of ourselves that we cannot access today. In a 1968 article, zoologist and author Desmond Morris

A dolphin boat tours Calibogue Sound.

Dolphins provide many opportunities for taking close-up photographs.

recalls his first visit to a zoo: "That visit did more for my later interest in animals than a hundred films or a thousand books. The animals were real and near. If zoos disappear, I fear the vast urban population will become so physically remote from animal life that they will eventually cease to care about it."

People are still seeking similar experiences with wild animals today. Each year, thousands of us seek dolphins on tours around Hilton Head Island. Are we looking for an experience of communion with a foreign (or not so foreign) consciousness? The African conservationist and author Geza Teleki experienced this as he watched a pair of chimps as *they* watched a stunning sunset over Lake Tanganyika. Later he wrote that the moment had "marked the twilight of my youth, I had seen my species inside the skin of another." It seems the more we learn about animals, the more they appear to be like us and we appear to be like them. The more we learn about dolphins, the more kindred our spirits.

Thirty-four of the seventy-nine species of cetaceans (whales, dolphins, and porpoises) belong to the family Delphinidae—the dolphins. Bottlenose dolphins, the species seen commonly in the waters around Hilton Head Island and the species most people picture when they hear the word *dolphin,* are found throughout the world in temperate and tropical waters. Research conducted over the last twenty years has resulted in huge leaps in our understanding of all aspects of bottlenose dolphin biology. Until recently, these advances were not readily available to the public, whose information lags decades behind the research. This book is a step toward bridging that gap, offering cutting-edge information to all those interested in learning more about dolphins. *The Dolphins of Hilton Head: Their Natural History* was written for the people drawn to Hilton Head and its dolphins, people who have seen and been touched by the dolphins.

This book is divided into three chapters. In the first, "Natural History of Hilton Head Dolphins," I define the term *marine mammal* and illustrate where Hilton Head dolphins fit into the global scheme of all marine mammals. Next, I detail the evolution of dolphin species and focus on the adaptations dolphins have made from an early terrestrial to aquatic environment. The life cycle of Hilton Head dolphins from birth through reproduction to death is outlined, and the chapter concludes with information on communication, echolocation, and intelligence. The second chapter, "Unique Characteristics of Hilton Head Dolphins," highlights the aspects of the dolphins that make them unique. I illustrate the relationships among environment, behavior, and social structure, focusing on the behaviors that the reader is likely to observe. The third chapter, "Dolphin Conservation," outlines the threats to local dolphins and the steps citizens can take to minimize their impact on dolphins and their fragile environment. In the two appendixes I answer commonly asked questions about dolphins and dispel some long-held dolphin myths. The bibliography provides related reading and websites.

ACKNOWLEDGMENTS

This book has materialized from initial conception in 1996 to the present form due to the input and efforts of innumerable friends, family, and colleagues. Many people have influenced its evolution in a variety of ways. Thanks to Barbara Owens for inspiring and encouraging me to write since I was a student in her high school freshman English class in 1978. Thanks to Fitz McAdden, executive editor of the *Island Packet,* for giving me the opportunity to hone my skills while writing about the natural wonders of the Hilton Head area for two years in a regular newspaper column. I enjoyed the learning and writing processes and benefited tremendously as a writer and a scientist. Thanks to Pamela Huntzinger, Erika Pusey, Becky Bittner, Dr. Ben Walker, Nancy Walker, and my family for their support during the writing of this book. Thanks to Brenda Gregory for her excellent illustrations that accompany and enhance the text. Vernell Dorner, Megan Cope, Marthajane Caldwell, Sue Barco, and Chris Eckland kindly reviewed earlier drafts of this book. Thanks to Carla Curran for her meticulous review of an earlier draft of this book. Jennifer Lewis and Peter Gubbins reviewed several drafts, and I appreciate their tireless efforts.

I first conceived of this book when I was beginning my dissertation research on the behavioral ecology of Hilton Head dolphins. Without the support I received on that project, this book would never have materialized. Therefore, I would like to acknowledge the individuals and organizations that supported my research and me during that time. I thank my dissertation advisor, Dr. Steve Jenkins, biology professor at the University of Nevada–Reno, for his contributions to my growth as a scientist and writer. Dr. David St. Aubin, director of research and veterinary services at Mystic Aquarium, was also a staunch supporter and helped me develop as a biologist. Palmetto Bay Marina generously donated dock space for my research vessel, the *Bubki.* In addition to being incredibly generous with logistical support, Harbormaster Chris Wimmer and Assistant Harbormaster Byron Bangs were wonderful friends who brightened my day whenever I saw them. I appreciate their interest in the dolphins and my research but am most deeply affected by their friendships. My research boat was owned by the South Carolina Nature Conservancy; thanks to Dale Soblo for facilitating our collaboration. Dr. Brenda McCowan, Dr. Diana Reiss, and Spencer Lynn helped me start this project and establish my research protocols and methods. Tom Murphy, Tom Doyle, Jana Moore, and the naturalists of the dolphin-watching company Commander Zodiac generously took time to introduce me to the area and to the local dolphins. Throughout my dissertation research, I was lucky to work with Tom Murphy, endangered species biologist for the South Carolina Department of Natural Resources. All aspects of my work and writing benefited from his input. I had the opportunity to work with many wonderful people while I was collecting data, all of whom volunteered their time and energy. I thank each of them; they were all great companions, tireless workers, and outstanding field assistants. Faculty and students at Eckerd College helped with several key analyses for my research. Kim Urian, curator for the *National Marines Fisheries Service Central Catalog,* and Marthajane Caldwell provided information on dolphins identified in South Carolina and Florida. Funding for my research was provided by the Worthington Foundation; the program in Ecology, Evolution and Conservation Biology; Mystic Aquarium; contributions of donors through Mystic Aquarium; and Tom and Sass Dodd. I received funding from the University of Nevada–Reno Graduate School, Biology Department, Graduate Student Association, and Program in Ecology, Evolution and Conservation Biology. My research was conducted under National Marine Fisheries Service General Authorization No. 2. All of the photographs in this book were taken while conducting research under this permit.

Neither my dissertation research nor this book would have been possible without the love and support of my family. I especially thank my husband, Chris Eckland, for his help on every aspect of both projects from conception to completion as well as his love, support, and friendship throughout the last eight years. Thanks to my dog, Iko, for her constant companionship during the writing of this book. Thanks to my dad, Peter Gubbins, for his love and encouragement and for his reviews of my dissertation and this book as a tireless, enthusiastic, and excellent editor. Thanks, too, to my wonderful mother, Donna Balsamo, whose love and friendship throughout my life helped me continually challenge myself and evolve as a human being.

THE DOLPHINS OF HILTON HEAD

CHAPTER ONE

NATURAL HISTORY OF HILTON HEAD DOLPHINS

Dolphins Are Marine Mammals

Dolphins swimming in the waters around Hilton Head Island are mammals who possess the defining characteristics of all mammals: they are vertebrates that breathe air with their lungs, are warm blooded, have hair at some stage of their lives, and bear live young who suckle milk secreted by mammary glands. A marine mammal spends most of its life at sea and exhibits physical and other adaptations to that environment. Mammals originally evolved on land but reinvaded marine realms on separate occasions to create the four main groups of marine mammals recognized today: *fissipeds* (sea otters and polar bears), *pinnipeds* (seals, sea lions, and walruses), *sirenians* (manatees and dugongs), and *cetaceans* (whales, dolphins, and porpoises). Their evolutionary relationships are illustrated in the figure below.

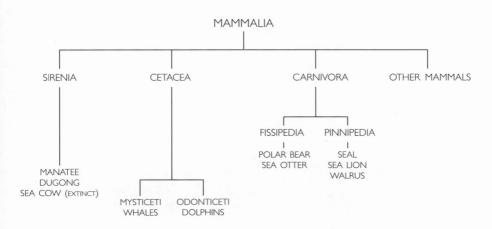

Evolutionary Relationships of Marine Mammals: Taxonomic relationships of the three distinct groups of marine mammals (sirenians, cetaceans, and carnivores). Each group evolved to an aquatic life independently from different evolutionary ancestors.

Sea otters and polar bears are fissiped (split-footed) mammals, evolutionary newcomers to the marine environment with the fewest anatomical and physiological adaptations. These mammals are more closely related to terrestrial carnivores such as weasels and bears, respectively, than to other marine mammals. Polar bears spend most of their life associated with marine water and ice. They rest, mate, give birth, and nurse on ice. However, sea otters rest, mate, give birth, and nurse their young in the water. Sea otters have no blubber; their fur insulates them from the heat-robbing water.

Pinnipeds (fin-footed) mammals are carnivores that have adapted to an amphibious marine life. They forage at sea and come onshore at various times of year to mate, give birth, nurse, or molt. Pinnipeds include the so-called earless seals (*phocids*), who lack external ears; the sea lions (*otariids*), who have external ears; and the walrus (*odobenids*), who lack external ears and have tusks.

Manatees and dugongs are the only living sirenians and are more closely related to elephants than to other marine mammals. The sirenians are completely aquatic herbivores. They live in tropical coasts, rivers, and estuaries. The Steller's sea cow went extinct within years of its discovery by humans; hunters quickly exterminated the slow-moving, docile sea cows.

The cetaceans (whales and dolphins) are also completely aquatic—they feed, mate, calf, and nurse in the water. Their closest relatives are the hippopotami. Cetaceans are the most specialized mammalian swimmers. One group of whales, also known as *mysticetes* or baleen whales, consists of filter feeders who exist on zooplankton and fish. They skim or gulp water with prey, then force the water out of their mouths through baleen plates, a kind of sieve that traps prey that are then swallowed. These are the largest animals to ever live on earth. The blue whale can be as large as 100 feet long and can weigh up to 125 tons. Toothed whales are known as *odontocetes*. This group includes dolphins, porpoises, beaked

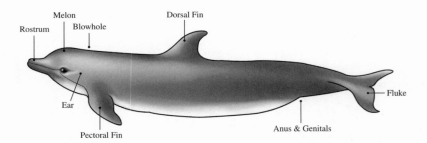

Bottlenose dolphins are streamlined aquatic mammals. Typical mammalian appendages have been modified over time for life in the water. This figure illustrates the external anatomy of a bottlenose dolphin.

whales, and sperm whales. Instead of baleen plates, they have identical conical or spade-shaped teeth for grasping prey. Odontocetes eat a wide variety of marine animals, mainly fish and squid.

Bottlenose dolphins are medium-sized marine mammals with smooth skin and torpedo-shaped bodies. They average 8 feet in length, but adults in different parts of the world range from 6 to 15 feet long and weigh 300 to 650 pounds. The bottlenose dolphin has a robust body with a dorsal fin, two pectoral fins, and a flattened tail called a fluke. Its mouth is a short, thick beak with many small, interlocking conical teeth, 40 to 52 on the upper jaw and 36 to 48 on the lower.

Dolphin coloration patterns have evolved to camouflage them from potential predators as well as from prey. The dorsal (top) surface is dark gray, lightening

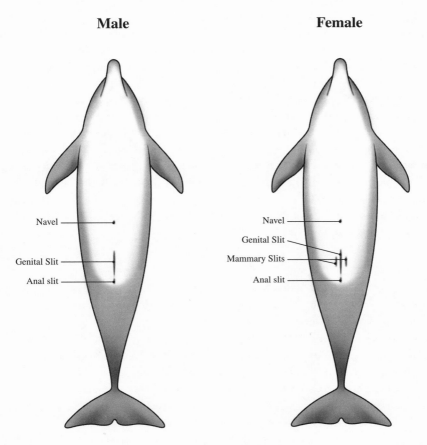

The gender of dolphins can be determined by the relative location of urogenital slits when they are visible. Males' two long slits are far apart; females have one long slit with a smaller mammary slit on either side.

along the sides to a white belly. This pattern is called countershading. When viewed from below, the white belly disappears into the bright surface of the water-air interface. When viewed from above, the darker dorsal surface blends into the dark depths of the ocean.

Because there is no obvious sexual dimorphism in this species (males and females do not differ significantly in size, and there are no obvious external differences), it can be difficult to determine the sex of a particular dolphin. But it can be done. One method is to view the genital slits on the dolphin's abdomen. Males have two slits in a line (a longer genital slit near the belly button and a shorter anal slit toward the tail), and females have a single urogenital slit in the center with a smaller mammary slit on each side. Viewing genital slits is no easy task under normal viewing conditions. Fortunately, males also can be identified by the observation of an erection, and females also can be recognized by a consistent, close association with a calf over several weeks or months. However, since dolphins other than mothers will often associate with a calf, one sighting with a calf is not enough to determine with certainty that the adult is the mother and therefore a female.

Dolphins are loosely grouped into three size categories that correspond to age, size, and social maturity. Neonates are newborn calves up to three months old and are less than one-third the size of an adult. Calves (generally three months to two years) are one-third to three-quarters the length of an adult. Full-sized animals can be juveniles (two years until sexually reproductive) or adults (reproductive or at least able to reproduce). Because subtle differences in size can be difficult to determine clearly in the field, a large dolphin who has not reproduced is considered an adult, as is a smaller dolphin that has reproduced (for example, a small female seen consistently with a calf).

Dolphin Evolution

More than thirty species of dolphins are recognized today. Why are there so many different kinds of dolphins? Each species has evolved slowly over several geological eras to adapt to different environmental conditions.

The evolution of all cetacean species has been related to two global environmental features: climate change and continental drift. These forces opened new habitats and made available new food resources for ancient animals. The first cetaceans (*archaeocetes,* or ancient cetaceans) began swimming about 55 million years ago during the Eocene period. Their predecessors had entered the warm, shallow waters of the Tethys Sea (of which the Mediterranean Sea is a remnant) to hunt fish. They thrived and gradually became less terrestrial and more aquatic.

During the Oligocene period, roughly 35 million years ago, the global temperature dropped drastically at the north and south poles, and deep currents of cold water began flowing from the poles toward the equator. Currents moving offshore were pulling deep water rich in nutrients up to the surface near the coast, a phenomenon known as upwelling. This rich water allowed many more plankton and fish to exist near the coasts, creating a new food source for aquatic mammals.

It is at this point that the archaeocetes began to change, and two different groups are believed to have begun their separate evolutionary paths to become modern mysticetes (baleen whales) and odontocetes (toothed whales). The first baleen whales (family Balaenidae, the right and bowhead whales), sperm whales, and beaked whales appear in the fossil record approximately 25 million years ago during the Miocene period. Five million years later, the river dolphins appeared in South America, India, and China.

The late Miocene (beginning 15 million years ago) saw the first narwhals and beluga whales. The delphinids first appeared in this period about 11 million years ago. Porpoises and the rorqual whales (baleen whales with throat grooves and dorsal fins in the scientific family Balaenopteridae) were close behind, arriving about 10 million years ago. The gray whale, according to the fossil record, is the youngest mysticete species at 5 million years old. The oldest known bottlenose dolphin fossils are two to 5 million years old. Bottlenose dolphin skeletons have been found in deposits from the Pleistocene epoch (2 million years ago) in Maryland and China.

Dolphin Adaptations

The earliest terrestrial dolphin ancestors probably walked on four legs and had long tails. These animals foraged near the water's edge, eventually spending more time in the water. Subsequent generations became completely aquatic, eventually evolving into the dolphins recognized today.

The most apparent dolphin adaptation is the streamlining of the body for swimming. Overall, the dolphin body has a fusiform shape—smooth and cylindrical like a bullet. All appendages have been reduced, right down to the disappearance of the external ear. Front legs have become pectoral flippers used for steering and controlling movement through the water. The hind limbs have been lost. A rudimentary pelvic girdle is all that remains of the ancestral cetacean's pelvis and hind legs. For propulsion in water, the tail and tailstock of modern cetaceans have increased musculature and a broad, flat area (fluke).

When researchers first began studying dolphin movement in the 1960s, they found dolphins to swim faster than what was believed to be physically possible. Scientists thought dolphins were defying the laws of physics. It took decades of intense study to discover many of the anatomical, physiological, and mechanical adaptations dolphins underwent to make them such fast, efficient swimmers. Unlike fish and sharks, which move their tails from side to side, cetaceans move their tails up and down. Dolphins get power from both the upstroke and downstroke of their tails, and the connective tissue around the tail muscles acts like a spring for fast, efficient swimming. Much like the kangaroo's tail, the dolphin's tail stores energy in its spring system. When the dolphin swims, it gets more energy (propulsion) out of tail strokes than it puts in via muscular contractions. This system allows the dolphin to expend less energy over the same distance than it would without the spring. The dorsal fin serves as a rudder, stabilizing the dolphin body and aiding in intricate underwater twists and turns.

While cetaceans still have whiskers around their rostrum at birth, a subcutaneous layer of fat has replaced the mammalian coat of fur. This layer allows for a more hydrodynamic body shape and provides insulation against the heat-drawing effect of water. The blubber also increases laminar (smooth, nonturbulent) flow of water around the body, enhancing speed and maneuverability. Even the dolphin skull is adapted for swimming: the cranial bones have flattened and lengthened (telescoping), and the nostrils have moved from the front of the face to the top of the head, becoming blowholes used for breathing.

The bodies of all warm-blooded mammals must maintain a relatively constant temperature to function properly. Water robs heat from a body forty times faster than air—a serious challenge for aquatic mammals. Dolphins therefore have developed several adaptations to regulate body temperature. The first is a large body

As dolphins have evolved to their aquatic lives, their bodies have adapted to maximize swimming efficiency. In a process called telescoping, dolphin heads have lengthened and flattened while the nostrils have migrated to the top of the head for efficient breathing while swimming.

Dolphins have excellent vision in and out of the water, probably have color vision, and can see in the low-light conditions underwater due to special adaptations of the eye.

with a low ratio of surface area to body volume. The less area exposed to the water, the slower the rate of heat loss. They use blubber for insulation and have complex configurations of veins and arteries to manage internal body temperature. These features allow the conservation and dissipation of heat as circumstances dictate.

Another challenge dolphins face living in the ocean is water conservation. Because dolphins have lower salt concentration in their blood and tissues than is present in the surrounding seawater, there is a tendency for water to leave their bodies in order to balance the internal and external concentrations. Dolphins cannot drink water to maintain their salt balance, so water conservation is as important to dolphins as it is to desert animals. Dolphins get all the water they need from ingested food, inspired air, and metabolized blubber. They also have specialized kidneys to produce urine that is saltier than seawater.

Aquatic living also presents special sensory challenges for marine mammals. An animal's senses allow it to receive and process information from its surroundings. When their evolutionary paths took them into the oceans, marine mammals had to adapt sensory systems that had evolved in air into ones that were able to detect and process signals in water. All marine mammal senses (vision, hearing, feeling, taste, and smell) have evolved to suit their aquatic lifestyle.

Dolphins have acute vision both in and out of water. Certain features of the lens and cornea correct for the different refractive properties of air and water. Without this adaptation, dolphins would be nearsighted in the air. Because the retinas of odontocetes have two central areas for receiving images (human eyes have only one), bottlenose dolphins have binocular vision in air and water (humans have monocular vision).

But a dolphin's eye is particularly adapted for seeing in water. Anatomical studies suggest dolphins might have both binocular and monocular vision underwater. A dolphin's retina contains both rods and cones, indicating the ability to see in dim and bright light. Rod cells respond to lower light levels than do cone cells. The presence of cone cells also suggests that dolphins may be able to see color, although studies on bottlenose dolphins have not confirmed this ability. A well-developed *tapetum lucidum,* a specialized cell layer at the back of the eye, reflects light through the retina a second time, thus enhancing vision in the dim light that is most prevalent underwater. Many nocturnal animals such as cats, also have this adaptation, revealed as eyes that seem to glow at night.

As a rule, light does not reach far into ocean water, so dolphins cannot rely primarily on their vision as terrestrial animals do. Dolphins therefore have evolved a sonar sense called echolocation that enables them to "see with sound." Clicks emitted from the melon (the fatty bulb of flesh on the forehead) bounce back to the dolphin when they strike an object. Dolphins send and receive many clicks per second to create a mental picture of their surroundings even in complete darkness. This process is detailed in the section titled "Echolocation."

As might be expected in animals that can see with sound through echolocation, dolphins have an acute sense of hearing. The auditory cortex—the part of the brain that controls hearing—is highly developed, and the auditory nerve has roughly twice as many fibers (67,900 or more) as does the human auditory nerve. Dolphins can hear sounds in a wide range of frequencies, from 1 to 150 kilohertz (kHz), but they hear best between 40 and 100 kHz. The human hearing range is about 0.02 to 17 kHz.

Hydrodynamic streamlining eliminated the external ear, the usual mammalian sound receptor, but dolphins hear very well. First, a dolphin has two small external ear openings, one slightly behind each eye. The openings lead to reduced ear canals and eardrums. Research indicates that these external ear openings receive sounds with frequencies below twenty kHz. Some researchers have concluded that these reduced ear openings are useful to dolphins; others believe that the external ear openings are nonfunctional and that other means account for sound reception.

The second way dolphins hear is through sound reception and conduction via the lower jaw. The lower jawbone is hollow and becomes broad where it hinges with the skull. This very thin bone extends back toward the auditory bulla, the bone that encases the inner ear. Fibrous tissues surround the auditory bulla, buffering the inner ear from the skull. Waterborne sounds are received most efficiently by specialized fat in the lower jaw. Fat extending from the jaw to the auditory bulla conducts the sound to the ear. The impulse is then conducted from the ear to hearing centers in the brain via the auditory nerve. This specialized hearing system, with broad sound receptors on each side of the head and isolated inner ears that receive sound from only one source, probably allows dolphins to localize sounds underwater quite effectively—a nearly impossible task for human swimmers.

The senses of touch, taste, and smell are less important to dolphins than are vision and hearing. However, dolphins are tactile animals and rub, nuzzle, and touch each other frequently. Anatomical studies indicate that their skin is sensitive to a broad range of tactile sensations, which supports researchers' belief that physical touching is an important factor in establishing and maintaining strong social bonds among dolphins.

Little is known about the dolphin sense of taste. Bottlenose dolphins have taste buds, and brain structure and cranial nerves suggest some sensation of taste. In the wild, dolphins' strong preferences for eating certain species of fishes might be related to taste. It is also possible that dolphins are able to taste the water they swim in, receiving information about other dolphins through hormones and pheromones released into the water. In this way, male dolphins may be able to determine the reproductive status of nearby females.

Hydrodynamic streamlining eliminated the dolphin's external ear; only a pinhole remains about an inch behind the eye. Although the ear is probably functional, dolphins receive sound mainly through their lower jaws.

Little is known about dolphins' sense of taste, but many researchers believe that dolphins can receive information about other dolphins through hormones and pheromones in the water sensed by their tongues.

If dolphins have any sense of smell, it is probably rudimentary, as the olfactory lobes of the brain and olfactory nerves are absent. Dolphin nostrils became blowholes over time and are probably used exclusively for breathing and not for smelling.

Efficient swimmers, dolphins regularly travel just under the water's surface. They can also dive to great depths to find food and avoid predators. Depending upon their habitat, they regularly make dives from 10 to 150 feet deep. The maximum depth recorded for a dolphin (in a controlled experiment) is 1,795 feet. Routine dives may last only a few minutes, but dolphins are able to stay underwater for up to ten minutes.

Dolphins have evolved several physical adaptations to overcome the challenges of deep diving. They use oxygen efficiently, routinely exchanging over 80 percent of the air in their lungs with each breath. Humans exchange only 17 percent. Dolphins also have high blood volume for their size, which enhances oxygen availability and use. Their blood has a high percentage of red blood cells, the cells that carry oxygen to the body. And dolphins have more myoglobin in their muscles than similarly sized terrestrial mammals, which allows for increased oxygen uptake from the blood. A high tolerance to lactic acid and carbon dioxide allow dolphins to maintain muscle activity while holding their breath.

Dolphins tolerate extreme water pressure at depth due to several specializations: most oxygen is stored in the blood and muscles, not in the lungs; their lungs and ribs are collapsible; their bodies have minimized air spaces; and their tissues allow only limited nitrogen absorption. These adaptations also prevent the "bends," a painful condition caused by compressed gas bubbles in the body expanding and bursting cells as depth and water pressure decrease. Scuba divers must regulate the rate of their ascents to the surface to avoid this ailment, but dolphins can freely dive to great depths and resurface at their own pace due to their physiological adaptations.

Dolphin Life

Although dolphins, like humans, can give birth at any time during the year, many dolphin populations have a birthing, or calving, season when most females give birth to their single infant. Water temperature, food availability, and lack of predators combine to determine when this optimal time occurs. The calving period in South Carolina occurs from May through July.

After a twelve-month gestation period, a female dolphin gives birth to a calf that is one-third to one-half her length. This is the equivalent of a five-foot woman giving birth to a thirty-inch baby. A newborn calf measures about four feet long and weighs roughly forty pounds. Unlike human babies, dolphin babies are born backward (tail first). Birth is initiated with uterine contractions while the mother floats at the water's surface with her tail hanging straight down or swims slowly in circles. As birth progresses, observers can see the mother's body bend in the middle, due to either the force of the contractions or initiated by the mother to

After a twelve-month gestation period, a female dolphin gives birth to a calf that is one-third to one-half of her length. The baby is born tail first and swims on its own to the surface for its first breath of air.

Newborn calves have fetal folds that look like vertical white stripes. Fetal folds result from uneven pigmentation while the calf is developing in the womb. These stripes fade a few weeks after birth.

facilitate birth. First, the baby's tail emerges, and the rest of the body follows. The umbilical cord breaks as the calf swims immediately to the water's surface for its first breath. The mother joins the baby and they swim together.

A dolphin birth near Hilton Head was witnessed by several kayakers who observed what appeared to be dolphin midwives helping the infant to the surface. I did not see this in the six dolphin births I observed in aquaria. When other dolphins were present at these births, they did not assist the birth and the calf swam on its own from the very instant of its birth, quickly beating its floppy little tail.

Neonates are easily recognized due to their small size (roughly one-third the length of the mother) and because they usually are much darker than adults, often appearing black. Because the baby is folded when in the womb, its pigmentation is different where the skin wrinkles; when first born, calves have "fetal folds," lightly colored vertical stripes. The stripes fade in a few weeks as the pigmentation evens out. Calves also can be recognized by their behavior: because they have more blubber than muscle, they tend to bob at the surface of the water like corks and are uncoordinated in their swimming and breathing. Very young calves must thrust themselves skyward straight out of the water, splashing down on their chins when they reach the surface, in order to keep their blowholes above water long enough to take a breath.

When born, dolphin calves are unable to swim very well or very fast, and it is not possible for them to keep up with adults. When with their mothers, calves most commonly stay right next to their mother's dorsal fin or under her belly. The first position, termed echelon position, is most common when the calves are quite young, between birth and six months. By positioning themselves next to the mother's dorsal fin, they get a free ride, like bicyclists drafting off each other. The baby is carried in the mother's slipstream with little or no swimming effort of its own. This hydrodynamic advantage allows dolphin mothers to "carry" their infants even at high speeds and is analogous to the way terrestrial mothers carry their young.

As calves develop more muscle and coordination, they can regulate their own swimming speed and buoyancy, allowing them to position themselves directly underneath the mother in the second mother-infant position. The underneath position is so common for mothers and calves that dolphin biologists call it the baby position. By staying under the mother's belly in the baby position, the infant realizes two benefits: easy access for nursing and camouflage from predators. Dolphin calves can spend up to 20 percent of the day nursing during their first year, so this position may be common simply because the baby is nursing so often. But dolphin calves are easy targets for predators and need extra protection. As in other species, most predators attack dolphin infants because they are easier to catch due to their lack of awareness, speed, and coordination. Sharks, dolphins' only natural predators, attack from below. As both infant and adult bellies are white, the dolphin baby blends into the mother's body when viewed from below, making the

Neonates are uncoordinated swimmers and can be recognized by their belly flops when they breathe. The rostrum points skyward as the baby dolphin thrusts its body straight out of the water and then crashes back down with a splash.

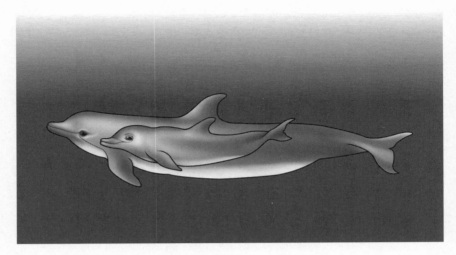

Mother and infant in echelon position. In this configuration, the baby is able to draft off the mother, staying with her with no effort even when she swims at her top speed. This position is most common from birth through six months of age when the infant has more fat than muscle and is not very strong or coordinated.

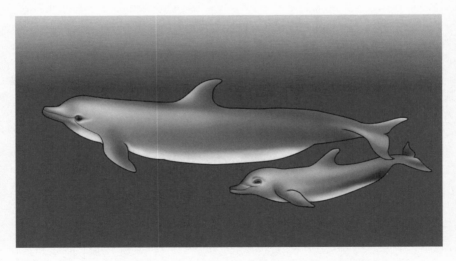

Mother and infant in baby position. This arrangement facilitates infant nursing and may be a social signal to other dolphins that the infant belongs to this mother. This position is more common when the baby is six months to several years old. Even after weaning, calves will return to their mother in this position when frightened or startled.

pair look like one large animal, and both blend into the bright surface of the water. Sharks are less likely to attack the calf either because it appears to be part of a larger animal or because the shark simply cannot see it.

A potential third benefit of the baby position is that it signals the mother-infant relationship to other dolphins. This position is more common than the echelon position when the baby is six months to several years old. Even after weaning, calves will return to the baby position when frightened or startled. This position may communicate to other dolphins that the infant has a large adult to protect it and even fight its battles. Most animals know not to disturb an angry mother. However, other calves and adults will also use this "baby" position when swimming together, making absolute interpretation tricky. Since pairs of calves, pairs of adult females, and mixed pairs of adult males and females have been observed in this position, researchers believe that it is a complex social signal that may indicate dominance hierarchies, appeasement, or a strong bond between pairs. This positioning may also simply illustrate the comfort zone of dolphins learned early in life while strongly attached to their mothers.

Dolphin mothers provide all of the nourishment, care, and protection that the baby needs. Nursing usually begins within six hours of birth. Calves nurse underwater, generally close to the surface, suckling from nipples concealed in their mother's abdominal mammary slits. A calf nurses as often as four times per hour throughout the day and night, with each nursing event usually lasting only about five to ten seconds. Rich dolphin milk is composed of 33 percent fat, 7 percent protein, and 58 percent water and enables the baby to rapidly develop strong muscles and a thicker layer of blubber. Calves commonly nurse for eighteen months or more, but infants may start experimenting with solid food by one year, and some start eating fish before their first birthday. The calves are not fully weaned until they are two to three years old, and females with calves often join to form nursery groups in which responsibility for guarding the vulnerable calves is shared. Male bottlenose dolphins do not provide any care for offspring.

Hilton Head might be a nursery area for both year-round dolphins (residents) and dolphins migrating along the east coast (transients). Some transient females may give birth and linger in the protected lowcountry marshes until the infants are able to travel long distances. Boaters should keep an eye out for babies: boats that approach too close will stress the new babies and their mothers. It is illegal to approach a dolphin within one hundred feet, so boaters are required to enjoy these new additions to the coastal neighborhood from a safe and respectful distance.

Independence comes late to these otherwise precocious mammals. Most calves do not leave their mothers until long after weaning, sometimes not until several

Dolphin calves commonly nurse for eighteen months or more but may start eating some solid food before their first birthday.

years later. Even after the calves are hunting and eating on their own, they stay with their mothers for several more months or even years. Some researchers have suggested that it takes this long to learn all the rules of this socially complex species, while others propose that additional learning is occurring: hunting techniques are perfected, and knowledge about the area's food supply and dangers is passed on. It is likely that both of these learning tasks contribute to the long post-weaning dependency of dolphin calves.

The juvenile years, between maternal independence and full sexual maturity, are spent mainly in the company of other juveniles. Some male dolphins will forge a lifelong bond with another juvenile male at this time. Although individual dolphins interact with many dolphins, the bonded male pairs will spend most of their time together for the next several decades. Females do not seem to form these strong bonds with an individual female; they spend most of their time with several females in juvenile and then adult groups. Juveniles occasionally return to visit their mothers during this period, but the intensity of their association diminishes, partly because the mother may have another baby to raise.

Male dolphins take longer to reach sexual maturity than females. Males are physically mature when they are eight to twelve years old, but it may take even longer for them to become socially mature and to mate with females. Females, on the other hand, are physically and socially mature between five and ten years of age.

Dolphin calves have an extended period of maternal dependency compared to other mammals. This difference may be due to the extensive learning they must undertake. A lot of learning is accomplished by watching adults hunt and interact.

Male and female bottlenose dolphins will mate with many partners over the course of their lives. Dolphins of both sexes choose their partners. Often females will arch their bellies out of the water to avoid mating with undesirable males.

The dolphin mating system is promiscuous, meaning that in a breeding season each male will mate with many females and each female will mate with many males. Mating commonly takes place in groups of three to ten dolphins, probably so that the male pairs together will find a single female with whom to mate. Often, pairs of males will join with other pairs to form coalitions. These coalitions in effect "kidnap" estrous females. The males surround the female, chasing her if she tries to escape, often vocalizing aggressively and biting her. Mating has not been observed when this happens, but researchers believe that males will isolate a female from her associates in order to mate with her later. This tactic ensures that the males will have exclusive mating access.

There is evidence that even within the male coalition-herding mating system, females still exercise their own choice in mating. Females can avoid mating by turning on their backs and arching their bellies out of the water. Pairs or groups of females will also join forces to escape confinement by male coalitions. However, being captured by the strongest males in the population may also be an expression of female mate choice. If a male has the social and physical skills to capture a female, he is likely to have very good genes, which the female would want to pass on to her offspring.

In some parts of the world, female dolphins return to their maternal group to raise their offspring, but this has not been verified for the Hilton Head area. It is generally believed that dolphins are able to reproduce for their entire adult lives.

Bottlenose dolphins average a twenty-year life span but can live for at least thirty and possibly more than fifty years.

Communication

Dolphins are social animals and regularly communicate with members of their group. For this communication, they employ a variety of mechanisms, both vocal and nonvocal. The selected method depends upon context, distance between dolphins, and environmental conditions. Although scientists recognize several modes of dolphin communication, it remains uncertain how many methods are used, how the communication systems are integrated, and whether dolphins employ a language similar to ours.

Most researchers believe that like humans, dolphins use a multilevel approach to convey information. In close range, they use body language and various visual displays to communicate. For example, an open-mouth show of teeth indicates a threat or a warning, and as the threat increases, the dolphin will add a head nod. Bubbles blown through blowholes indicate surprise, excitement, or agitation. Bursts of large bubbles warn of serious threats. The ultimate warning posture of a dolphin is called the *S* position, in which the dolphin lowers its head and tail and arches its back to form an *S*. If warnings are not heeded, a head-on attack is likely. During attacks, dolphins will rake each other with their teeth and even bite.

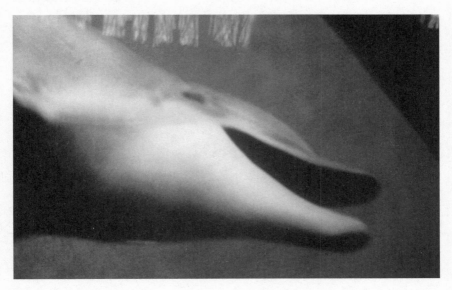

Dolphins communicate with body language and visual displays. An open mouth indicates mild displeasure or a low-grade threat. If this warning is not heeded, more serious behavior will follow.

A head-on attack follows several other warning signals increasing in intensity from an open mouth to showing the teeth to head nods to bubble bursts.

Strongly bonded dolphins often swim side by side with pectoral fins touching, possibly to project feelings, much like hand-holding among humans.

Body language is another important mode of dolphin communication. Using their bodies as percussive instruments, dolphins can communicate by slapping their tails and bodies on the water surface. The combination of noise production and water displacement conveys information to dolphins that might be hundreds of yards away. Many subtle body movements, often unnoticed by human observers, can indicate an intention to change behavior. Reading and reacting to these cues leads to synchronous group behavior, whether the behavior is traveling together to a new foraging site or quickly fleeing from a predator. The ability to read group members' body language allows dolphins to coordinate their movement and behavior and to maintain group cohesiveness, staying together even in difficult circumstances. Flocks of birds and herds of ungulates (hoofed mammals such as horses, cattle, elephants, and pigs) use subtle cues in a similar way to coordinate their behavior. Body language can also change the context of other types of communication. Posture can indicate that whatever is happening is not to be taken seriously, as in play fighting, or can lend emphasis to communication, as in aggressive vocal exchanges coupled with vigorous head-bob warnings.

Physical contact can also convey information. Strongly bonded dolphins often will swim side by side with a pectoral fin touching, possibly to project feelings, much like our hand-holding. Rubbing fins or bodies appears to convey information about emotions or the status of relationships. And it is considered possible that dolphins use echolocation, which has a sensory component, to convey personal information and feelings, in a manner similar to our use of touch.

The most important communication method for dolphins is vocalization. Sounds are effective at great distances and in low-visibility situations such as at night or in murky water. Dolphins produce sounds by moving air through nasal air sacs and passages. These sounds are projected through their melons—the fatty bulb on their foreheads. Vocalizations can be whistles, pure sounds similar to bird songs, or burst pulse sounds such as squawks, yelps, bleats, and thunks. Whistles are used in several contexts and probably communicate many kinds of information. Burst pulse sounds are generally used in intense social interactions such as fighting and mating. It is speculated that these types of sounds might convey more emotion than information.

Dolphins clearly have the ability to communicate with each other, but as scientists learn more, they are increasingly challenged to understand the complete communication system. Anecdotal evidence suggests that dolphins can convey precise information as well as relate events and emotions. Many scientists believe that understanding dolphin communication will enlarge our knowledge of the evolution of human language.

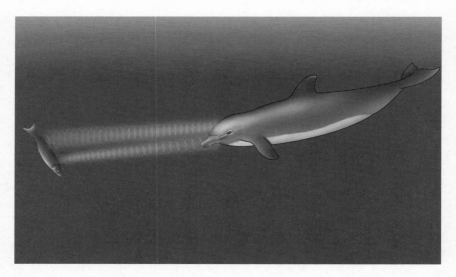

Dolphins use their echolocation sonar to see with sound. A stream of clicks is sent out from the melon. When the clicks hit an object, they return to the dolphin, who is able to interpret the information and make a mental picture of the object.

Echolocation

Humans rely on five senses (sight, touch, hearing, taste, and smell) to get information about the world around us, but dolphins also use an "extra" sense: echolocation—the ability to use sound to see.

Echolocation works in a deceptively simple way. The dolphin emits a directed sound wave called a click from its melon. Each click lasts about 50 to 128 microseconds. The sound wave travels through the water at a speed of 0.9 miles per second, which is 4.5 times faster than sound traveling through air. When it encounters objects such as fish, rocks, and other dolphins, the sound wave bounces off and returns to the dolphin as an echo. The dolphin receives the echo in its lower jaw, which transmits the information via the specialized fat within it to the inner ear and then to the auditory center in the brain. An acoustic image of the environment or a specific object is then created. For greater detail, the dolphin emits a series of clicks, called a click train, at a higher frequency. Dolphins and other odontocetes use this system to determine size, shape, speed, distance, direction, and even some of the internal structure of objects in the water. Echolocation provides dolphins the ability to discriminate so sensitively that two species of fish can be distinguished, even if they are the exact same size.

Longer wavelengths and greater energy allow low frequency sounds to travel farther through water than high frequency sounds. Because it is a relatively high frequency sound, echolocation is most effective at close to intermediate range, about 16 to 656 feet, when discriminating objects 2 to 6 inches in length.

Dolphins can communicate and even eavesdrop on each other with echolocation. In foraging groups, the rhythms of the click trains indicate the location of other group members, their activities, their distance to prey, and perhaps even the prey species.

Echolocation clicks have such a strong energetic component that they have a tactile aspect. Other dolphins can feel echolocation clicks as a gentle caress or a powerful punch, depending upon their strength. Some scientists believe that dolphins can also create an exceptionally forceful echolocation pulse, called a big bang, to stun and debilitate fish and make them easier to catch and eat.

Unlike human sense of hearing, echolocation must be learned by young dolphins through observation and practice. It is likely that females actively teach their young how to echolocate. Dolphin calves can echolocate with their mouths open by the time they are four weeks old, and by five weeks they can echolocate with a closed mouth. Biologists cannot explain why calves begin echolocating with an open mouth and then switch to a closed mouth. The skill is developed and refined as calves age, but researchers do not know at what age a dolphin's echolocation apprenticeship is finished. Researchers also do not know how long it takes to learn to interpret echolocation information. For instance, when is a fish recognized as food rather than simply an object in the environment, such as a rock? The echolocation clicks of a calf start to look like adult clicks when visualized on a spectrogram when the calf is about six weeks old; after that, the dolphin continues to perfect its sixth sense for the rest of its life.

Echolocation is an active sense: dolphins must use it consciously. Thus, echolocation "hearing" and "seeing" is not always "on." This may be one of the reasons that dolphins become accidentally entangled in fishing gear. It may be that they have the ability to detect the gear but they are not always "looking" for it and therefore get tangled in it.

Intelligence

In the 1960s, the psychologist and author Dr. John Lilly predicted that humans would have meaningful communication with another species before the year 2000. The creatures he thought most likely to talk back to humans were the dolphins, who he believes are at least as smart as humans. This appealing idea captured our collective imagination, and the intelligence of dolphins is now widely considered indisputable. But what exactly is intelligence, and do dolphins truly possess it?

For our purposes, intelligence can be defined simply as the capacity to acquire and apply knowledge. The scientific community has devised many intricate tests to measure human intelligence and to rank our intelligence against that of other people and species. Dolphins have come out on top in most cases.

Brain size was the first test employed, demonstrating that dolphins have very large brains. But brain size is often correlated with body size—large animals have large brains simply due to their overall size. Using the ratio of brain size to body size avoids this connection. On this scale, dolphins rank above all other animals and just below humans.

Another test is the extent of folding in the brain, called convolution. Convolution creates more surface area in the same amount of space, allowing more information to be processed. Dolphins surpass all other animals, including humans, on this scale. But dolphin brain tissue is not very thick, so some researchers doubt that their extensive convolution warrants top honors in the intelligence contest.

The ability of a member of an animal species to recognize itself has been long considered a sign of intelligence, mainly because humans can do it but most animals cannot. This test is usually conducted with a mirror, in which the animal can see a spot of color applied on its body that it could not see in any other way. Animals must react to the mirror-assisted knowledge of the spot in specific ways in order for researchers to believe that they possess self-awareness. Chimpanzees do well with this test, although most monkeys do not. Dolphins do seem to be able to use mirrors to recognize themselves.

Tool use, the ability to manipulate a foreign object for a specific purpose, is another interspecies intelligence test. Humans and other primates, with hands designed for grasping, top this scale. But handless dolphins also use tools, and they are adept at manipulating their environment. Some dolphins in Shark Bay, Australia, have been observed putting sponges on their snouts as they forage, probably to protect them from stings of fish they are rooting out of the mud. Captive dolphins have taken feathers floating in their tanks and used them to poke eels, scaring the eels from their refuges in rock tunnels.

Dolphin communication is widely considered another hallmark of their intelligence. Captive dolphins have been taught to use several artificial "languages" to communicate with researchers, including hand gestures, computer-generate whistles, and visual symbols on underwater "blackboards." Results of research conducted at the Kewalo Basin Marine Mammal laboratory in Honolulu show that dolphins responding to gestured commands use syntax as humans do, discriminating, for example, between a command to place a hoop on a surfboard and a command to place a surfboard on a hoop. These dolphins also can generalize concepts: a "ball" is recognized whether it is red or blue, large or small.

But it should be kept in mind that all these tests measure only how humanlike an animal is, not how intelligent. After all, humans set the scales and generally base them on ways that people express intelligence. If we define intelligence as the capacity to acquire and apply knowledge, dolphins and many other animals must be deemed "intelligent."

By nearly any standard, including the ultimate test of survival in an unpredictable and dangerous environment, dolphins can be considered intelligent. They are quick learners, have good memories, and apply new knowledge in novel situations. And perhaps most telling of all: anecdotes told by dolphin trainers and researchers suggest that dolphins have a sense of humor.

CHAPTER TWO

UNIQUE CHARACTERISTICS OF HILTON HEAD DOLPHINS

Perhaps as a natural aspect of biophilia (E. O. Wilson's theory of human attraction to other animals), humans are insatiably curious about the animals around us. This natural curiosity has benefited from the development of a logical format for formal scientific inquiry, commonly known as the scientific method. The scientific method is quite simple: First, selected subjects are watched and specific questions are developed, then these questions are put in the form of testable hypotheses. Next, the subjects are observed again, and this time specific pieces of information relevant to the questions and hypotheses are recorded. After analyzing the data, the results are interpreted and put in perspective based on what is already known about the subject.

Dolphins have been studied in this way for decades, first as captives in aquaria and marine parks and then, as technology allowed, in their natural habitat.

Dolphin dorsal fins can look very similar. Often, detailed examination of dorsal fin photos with a magnifying glass is necessary to make a confident identification.

Hook is one of the roughly four hundred dolphins that inhabit Hilton Head waters year round. She was fed when dolphin feeding was legal, but she likely resumed her natural feeding habits when the fish handouts significantly decreased following the ban on feeding in 1996.

Scientists studying dolphins in the wild face special challenges as dolphins spend over 90 percent of their lives underwater. Hard-won glimpses into dolphins' lives have been remarkably informative; most of what we know about dolphins comes from information so gleaned.

The precise methods depend upon the goals of the study and the specific questions. Questions about population size can be answered by counting dolphins in a predetermined fashion from land or from a boat or airplane. Relative abundance of dolphins can be measured by comparing the numbers of dolphins seen in different locations or at different times of the year, for instance. These two examples represent short-term studies.

Long-term studies require a researcher to follow dolphins for periods of time ranging from a few months to several years. Long-term research has provided information on population size, ranging patterns, daily and seasonal movements, social structure, behavioral ecology, calf development, and communication. The first step in any long-term study is to identify individuals. Like human skin, a dolphin's skin will scar after being cut or scraped; these scars can be used by researchers to identify individuals. Scars are caused by encounters with sharp objects, shark attacks, boat collisions, and even by one dolphin scraping another dolphin with its sharp teeth. Scars can be permanent or can disappear after a few weeks or months. Other marks such as pigmentation concentrations (like freckles) or other variations in coloration can be also distinctive. Some are permanent while others might not last long enough for identification. It might require several sightings of an individual dolphin to tell if a mark is reliable.

Although scars and other marks can be helpful in recognizing individuals, dolphin researchers primarily use photographs of dolphin dorsal fins to identify and reidentify individual dolphins over seasons and years. Dolphin dorsal fins vary in shape and size and remain relatively unchanged after several years. The researcher photographs the dorsal fin from a lateral angle, and this photograph is then compared to a catalog of photos of the dorsal fins of recognized individuals. If a new fin photo matches one in the catalog, this is a resighting of a known dolphin. If there is no match, a new individual has been identified. Two fins can be very similar, making objective comparisons imperative.

Each researcher builds a personal catalog of dolphin fin prints, but researchers in nearby areas often will compare catalogs to investigate movements of individuals. Several independent researchers along the east coast meet each year for this purpose and together have amassed a master fin catalog that includes nearly three thousand individual dolphins from New Jersey to Florida.

Photo-identification studies in the Hilton Head area have been used to determine population size, ranging patterns, daily and seasonal movements, social structure, and behavioral ecology. Using this method in my own research, nearly five hundred individual dolphins in the Hilton Head area have been identified. I was able to follow some individuals from the first day of research to the last, four and a half years later. About fifty of these dolphins are year-round residents, and the rest are transients moving through the area, staying for varying lengths of time. Use of scientific formulas based on the rate of identifying and resighting individuals over several months determines that there are fewer than four hundred residents and at least two thousand other individuals in Hilton Head waters.

Bottlenose dolphins inhabit seas and oceans all over the world, but dolphins are not all the same. Dolphin lives, like those of all wild animals, are interwoven with the fabric of their environment. Different populations can differ greatly in their social structure and behavior due mainly to environmental variation. The scientific field of behavioral ecology developed from this truism. The word "ecology" is derived from Greek roots meaning "house" (*oikos*) and "study of" (*ology*). So behavioral ecology is the interpretation of animal behavior in the context of the animal's environment, or where it lives. This field encompasses all aspects of animal behavior, from movement and migration patterns to ranging, foraging, and social behavior.

Movement Patterns

In the western Atlantic Ocean, bottlenose dolphins are common from Argentina's north coast to New England. Along the Atlantic coast of the United States, they can be seen from the Florida Keys to Long Island. The two types of bottlenose dolphins recognized in most parts of the world, coastal and offshore, are also found here in the western Atlantic Ocean. Offshore dolphins are concentrated near the continental shelf, thirty-five to one hundred twenty-five miles off the coast, from the Gulf of Mexico to Nova Scotia, while coastal dolphins stay generally within several miles of land.

Coastal dolphins are observed as far north along the east coast as New York, but distribution patterns of the coastal dolphins change seasonally along the eastern seaboard. In the summer, coastal dolphins are found from Florida to New York, but their numbers are greatest between North Carolina and New Jersey. In the fall, dolphin abundance drops dramatically between New York and Virginia, with only a handful of sightings of a few individuals being reported during winter months over the last several decades. Dolphin density increases northward along the coast again in the spring, although the southern end of the range remains occupied. This regular pattern of shifting dolphin abundance suggests that at least part of the coastal segment of the Atlantic bottlenose dolphin population undertakes

Over three hundred of the several thousand transient dolphins who move through Hilton Head waters have been identified. This dolphin is an adult female who was also identified by researchers in Jacksonville.

regular seasonal migrations along the coast. Coastal dolphins spotted from Virginia to New York in the summer likely migrate south along the coast and spend the winter at the southern end of their range between Cape Hatteras and central Florida. Because not all the coastal dolphins join the migration, these dolphins are currently thought to be comprised of two distinct groups: coastal migratory and coastal resident.

In the Hilton Head area, both year-round residents and seasonal migratory residents, or transients, are seen. The transient dolphins are generally present between May and October, but individuals stay in the area for only several days at a time. Resident dolphins, on the other hand, remain throughout the year. Several thousand transient dolphins are thought to roam the coastline along the east coast of the United States, while fewer than four hundred resident dolphins live in the Hilton Head area.

Foraging Behavior

For dolphins living in an unpredictable environment, feeding (consuming captured fish) is one of the most, if not *the* most, important survival behavior. During my study, I observed dolphins foraging (looking for and attempting to capture fish) more often than any other type of behavior. Hilton Head dolphins spend nearly half their day foraging or feeding. Not all hunting efforts are successful, so more

Dive depth can be inferred from dolphin surface behavior. A tail-up dive indicates the dolphin is making a steep dive, will likely be swimming to deeper depths, and will remain underwater for a long time.

A tail-stock dive, with only part of the tail showing, indicates a dolphin is making a shallow dive.

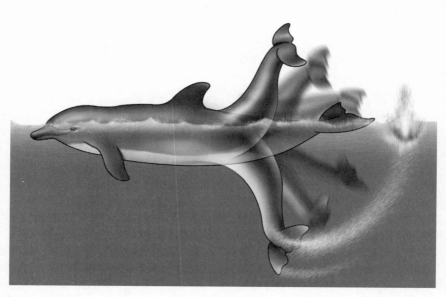

A dolphin slaps the surface of the water with the ventral surface of its tail, dragging the tail down through the water column. This action apparently stuns prey, which are then captured. This foraging behavior can be performed singly or synchronously by pairs of dolphins.

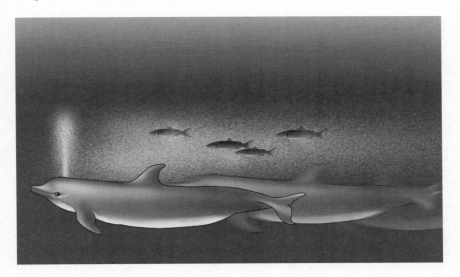

Two or more dolphins move past a school of fish emitting a stream of small bubbles that rise to the surface, creating a wall on two sides of the fish school. Individual dolphins take turns moving through the school to capture one fish at a time.

time is spent foraging then actually feeding. Social interaction, travel, and resting fill the rest of the dolphins' day.

Dolphins in the Hilton Head area are innovative hunters, utilizing a wide variety of foraging behaviors to capture many species of fish. Unlike humans, who have hands and use a variety of tools, dolphins appear to be without the means to manipulate their environment, but Hilton Head dolphins use many tools to help them obtain prey: anatomical functions, including sonar to detect and stun prey; tails to trap and debilitate prey; bubble streams to surround and corral fish; underwater creek walls and tidal currents to herd fish; and even mudbanks to strand fish out of water for easier capture. Some of these tactics have been observed only in the Hilton Head area.

The most common local feeding behavior is single feeding, in which a dolphin will focus its hunting efforts on one individual fish. When single feeding, a dolphin surfaces erratically in varying directions in roughly the same area over several minutes. Often two or more dolphins will be single feeding near each other, but their efforts are uncoordinated and each is hunting independently. Dolphins in all habitats use this foraging behavior. Bottlenose dolphins prey on a variety of fish that are found at varying water depths. Dolphins adjust the depth of foraging dives to hunt specific prey; their surface behavior can indicate their intended diving behavior. When a dolphin dives, the amount of tail seen and the degree of body arch can be used as indicators of the depth of the dive. The more tail seen as

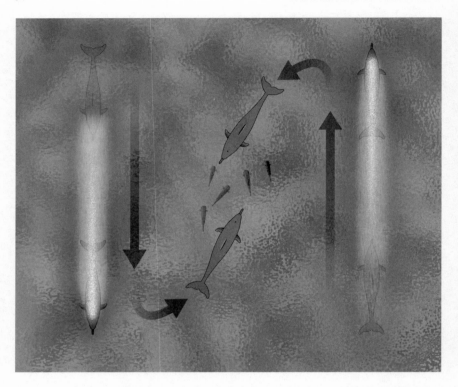

Two dolphins synchronize their movement past a school of fish, starting the pass at opposite corners of the school. Bubbles are emitted as the pass begins, and the bubbles stop when the dolphins reach the periphery of the school.

the dolphin dives, the deeper the dive will be and the longer the dolphin is likely to stay underwater. A tail-up dive indicates the dolphin is headed straight down, making a deep dive. Rolling dives, showing only the dorsal fin and back, are generally short and shallow.

Bottom feeding is another common foraging behavior. Dolphins eat many species of bottom-dwelling fish, including a few that burrow under sand or mud. Locating the buried fish with echolocation, the dolphins bury their rostrums in the mud or sand. In shallow water, their tails stick straight up out of the water and wave back and forth, making this behavior easy to recognize. Dolphins bottom feed alone, as in single feeding, but groups of dolphins often can be seen individually bottom feeding near each other in shallow and deep water. If a dolphin's rostrum is covered in mud, it likely has been bottom feeding.

In the backwaters of tidal creeks, dolphins use a pinwheel action to catch small prey near the water's surface. A single dolphin chases its prey at the water's surface

One or more dolphins releases large bursts of air bubbles around the periphery of a school of fish. Individuals take turns moving through the school to capture prey.

in a tight circle while positioned on its side. The entire dolphin is visible at the surface, and usually one pectoral fin sticks up out of the water. Groups of two or three dolphins will use this tactic near each other, with each one tracking and catching its own prey. Pinwheeling is commonly seen in winter and spring when the prey is at the water's surface.

Using the action of receding tides is one of the clever tools Hilton Head dolphin groups have used to help catch their dinner. When tidal feeding, one or several dolphins will remain stationary facing upstream at the mouth of a tidal creek, capturing fish as they are swept out of the creek with the falling tide. If dolphins are seen next to each other in a line facing into a creek, chances are they are feeding on the fish moved by the tides. This behavior is common where small tidal creeks empty into Calibogue Sound. Perhaps the creeks are steeper, moving fish quickly toward the waiting dolphins, or it may be that the fish are concentrated at the narrow creek mouths and the dolphins maximize their meal as the water collects fish from far up many tiny, connected creeks at one location before the creeks open into the larger sound and ocean. By lining up abreast at the creek mouth, the dolphins work together to limit the avenues of escape.

These are all straightforward feeding behaviors that individuals can perform alone, but local dolphins are innovative when working together to maximize their foraging efficiency. An example of cooperative foraging is circle feeding. Two or more dolphins work together, moving in a circle around a school of prey, usually

*Dolphins feed on prey disturbed by nets dragged behind the shrimp boat, prey caught in
the nets, bycatch thrown overboard, or fish attracted to the anchored shrimp boat when
the shrimpers are sorting catch and disposing of unwanted fish.*

mullet. The circling action keeps the fish bunched tightly together as the dolphins
take turns dashing through the center of the school to catch individual fish. Yet
another method is group feeding, in which two or more dolphins coordinate
foraging efforts but do not circle the school of prey. Often individual dolphins position themselves on opposite sides of a school and take turns catching fish in the
group.

Dolphins' amazing control over their body movements is demonstrated in a
strategy in which a dolphin slaps the surface of the water with the ventral surface
of its tail, dragging the tail down through the water column. By dragging its tail,
the dolphin creates a loud noise as well as a column of bubbles rising to the surface. A large splash of water jets upward immediately following the tail slap,
creating a "kerplunk" sound. The force of the slap or the bubble column or both
stun the prey, which is then captured. This behavior has been observed only in the
tidal creeks, so it may require relatively shallow water. Often, two dolphins will
perform tail kerplunks at the same time, synchronizing the tail slap.

In one of their most innovative foraging tactics, Hilton Head dolphins use
bubbles to trap or confuse their prey. Two different tactics are used: creation of a
wall of fine, small bubbles or encirclement of the school with large bubbles released
simultaneously. In the first strategy, two dolphins move past a school of fish at the
same time, starting from opposite sides, simultaneously emitting a string of small
bubbles that rise to the surface. The bubbles create two parallel walls on either

side of the fish school. When they reach the periphery of the school, each dolphin takes a turn moving through the school to capture prey. Dolphins use this tactic in Calibogue Sound. In the second strategy, one or more dolphins circle the fish, releasing large air bubbles at intervals around the school. In a group of dolphins, the bubbles are expelled at roughly the same moment, temporarily trapping the fish. Each individual takes a turn moving through the school to capture prey. Dolphins in quiet tidal creeks use this method.

Dolphins in tidal creeks also use underwater geological features to help them capture prey. When barrier feeding, dolphins take advantage of the steep underwater walls of the creek to help them herd schools of fish for easier capture. By circling the school in front of a wall, the dolphins decrease potential escape routes. Dolphins also use the shallow water feeding technique, swimming on their sides in water less than three feet deep. This technique is performed both individually and in groups of two or more dolphins. In a group, all the dolphins face and travel in the same direction within a body length of each other. Fish are trapped in the shallow water over sandbars or even just out of the water on dry sandbars as the dolphins remain in the shallow water.

Strand-feeding dolphins create a wall of water in front of them as they rush onto the land.

Fish are carried by the force of the wave and deposited on the land when the wave breaks.

Local dolphins will also exploit human fisheries to make hunting easier. Dolphins regularly can be seen feeding behind shrimp boats as their nets troll the waters for groups of shrimp. These dolphins will eat fish caught in nets, bycatch thrown overboard, and fish disturbed on the bottom by the dragging nets. Some dolphins will also follow crab boats as the fishermen travel local waterways retrieving crabs and replacing the fish bait in the crab traps. These dolphins often receive the retrieved bait or even a crab thrown to them by the fishermen.

Perhaps the most dramatic, and dangerous, foraging method used by local dolphins is strand feeding, so called either because the dolphins appear to strand themselves on land temporarily or because the prey are stranded on the land. The dolphins throw themselves out of the water onto the mudflats, pushing a wall of water in front of them. Fish in this moving wall of water are left flopping on the mud, then gulped by the beached dolphins. The dolphins then slip backward into the water and soon reappear in an explosive burst of water on another bank. While on the mudbank, the dolphin risks getting stuck on the land. Strand-feeding dolphins occasionally slide completely out of the water, making the return to the water more difficult. Unable to simply push itself free with arms or legs, the dolphin must wriggle and turn its body, inching backward toward the water. A dolphin caught on land faces the risks of sunburn, crushed internal organs, and, ultimately, death. The strand-feeding technique is used by single dolphins and by groups of two to six dolphins. In a group, the dolphins precisely coordinate the landward rush so that all group members emerge from the water at the same time. Each dolphin eats the fish it can reach and then slides back into the water independently of others in the group.

Along the east coast, strand feeding can be observed only in the tidal creeks and marshes of South Carolina and Georgia and only during a window of a few hours around low tide when conditions are exactly right. Bottlenose dolphins in Texas, Louisiana, and Portugal have also been observed strand feeding. Humpback dolphins in South Africa and killer whales in Argentina use similar strategies when hunting fish and seal pups, respectively.

It is not known what signals, if any, the dolphins use to coordinate their drive onto the land. It may be that the dolphins are not coordinating their foraging effort at all. No one has observed any definitive physical signal that always precedes strand feeding, nor has any acoustic signal (whistles or echolocation clicks) been reliably associated with strand feeding. There might be a producer-scrounger effect: one dolphin initiates the rush, judging the correct place and time, and near-by dolphins, with their quick reflexes, simply follow the leader.

Two dolphins strand feeding together can make a bigger wave as they rush the shore, thus beaching more fish in the process. This mutualism (both participants benefit from the association with the other) suggests that cooperation likely is involved. Many scientists argue that if food is shared, then the foraging is cooperative. Researchers do not know if the dolphins are sharing in the altruistic sense of giving up one's own opportunity to eat so that a companion can eat; it may be that each dolphin takes all fish within its reach as fast as possible, in a competitive way.

Dolphins beach themselves on land as they snatch fish from the mud. The dolphins risk sunburn, crushed internal organs, and even death if they remain on land too long.

Strand-feeding dolphins ingest fine mud along with the fish. Teeth on the right sides of their mouths are often worn by the grinding effect of the mud.

Dolphins strand feed alone or in groups of up to six dolphins. After capturing the fish, dolphins slide back into the water tail first, or they turn around and re-enter the water head first.

Social Structure

For bottlenose dolphins, it is impossible to consider behavior apart from environmental and social features. The social group into which a dolphin is born largely determines the course of the rest of its life. A dolphin is more likely to encounter other community members than nonmembers and form bonds and alliances with these individuals. Communities are often formed around environmental features such as connected waterways, and within these areas environmental conditions may be very specialized, even determining what the dolphins will eat and how they will be able to locate and capture their food.

Bottlenose dolphins have a complex social structure that is similar to those of humans and chimpanzees; many relationships are maintained for years, even decades, but countless other interactions are fleeting. This social complexity is thought to be responsible for the evolution of dolphins' large brains and intelligence. The precise nature of the social structure of each dolphin population depends upon local environmental and other conditions. In some areas, females inhabit small areas while males roam among the ranges of many different females. In other areas, males and females regularly travel long stretches of coastline in large groups, which can exceed one hundred individuals.

The social structure of Atlantic bottlenose dolphins along the entire U.S. east coast reflects two distinct environmental features: the long coastline of the eastern edge of North America and the bays, inlets, and estuaries that punctuate it. Open

Two strongly bonded dolphins, either a mother and her calf or two adult or juvenile males, comprise the smallest social unit in bottlenose dolphin societies. Strongly bonded pairs often perform synchronous leaps.

Choppy, a year-round resident dolphin most often seen in Calibogue Sound, belongs to the Sound community.

coastlines are correlated with large, roaming communities of dolphins with fluid social associations and little fidelity to any particular area; inlets such as bays and estuaries are generally populated by smaller, tightly knit communities with strong site fidelity—the dolphins tend to be resident in one area year round. Many over-lapping resident and transient dolphin communities comprise the coastal Atlantic bottlenose dolphin population.

The social organization of Hilton Head dolphins reflects the local geographic and environmental features. Small, tight communities of year-round residents are seen in the inland estuaries and creeks and together form the resident dolphin population. These communities generally restrict their ranges to small areas defined by geological features such as tidal creeks and rivers. The larger, transient popu-lation inhabits both coastal and inland waters, potentially travels the length of the eastern seaboard from Florida to New York, and may consist of several different transient communities. Residents and transients use the same waters in Calibogue Sound, and many of the tidal creeks and rivers, occasionally interact-ing with each other. This social organization, with distinct populations of station-ary and roving individuals that share one location, is rare among bottlenose dol-phins (and among all mammals for that matter).

Dolphins in a community share similar home-range geography, tend to employ similar foraging behaviors, and have stronger associations with other community members than they do with nonmembers. There are several levels of social organ-ization within a community; each higher level is characterized by lower association

Chip is a member of the Creek community. He has been observed strand feeding in Bull Creek.

rates among the individuals. The smallest social unit is the mother-calf pair with high association rates, near 100 percent (always seen together) for the first few years of the calf's life. Pairs of males also form long-lasting bonds with association rates between 50 and 100 percent for their adult lives. Next up the scale are nursery groups of several mother-calf pairs that associate together regularly but have association rates lower than 50 percent. Social, foraging, and mating groups form less regularly, and individuals in these groups generally have lower association rates than nursery groups. Together, these levels of relationships form a community. Not all dolphins within a particular community will interact, and members of one community will occasionally interact with members of neighboring communities.

Within every community of dolphins around Hilton Head Island, each dolphin has its own home range, the area it traverses for normal activities such as finding food and mates and caring for young. These home ranges overlap to varying degrees within a community but rarely overlap those of dolphins in nearby communities. Because dolphins are not territorial, some home ranges can completely overlap each other. This is especially true for male pairs, who tend to spend the majority of their time together. In the waters surrounding Hilton Head Island, individual resident dolphins rarely travel outside their home ranges and are never seen in the open ocean. The size of these home ranges varies from thirty-five to fifty square miles. Hilton Head dolphins have core-use areas where they spend the majority of their time, but they also move around extensively within their home ranges as they search for food and interact with their neighbors. Core-use areas

Transient dolphins are usually seen in larger groups than resident dolphins.

are probably features of all coastal bottlenose dolphin home ranges, but to date
this phenomenon has been studied only among Hilton Head dolphins. Certain
areas within a home range also appear to be used for different activities, for example, feeding in one area, socializing in another, and resting in a third. This divi-
sion of a home range is not surprising, since the marine environment around
Hilton Head Island is extremely variable with different locations forming an
underwater mosaic of distinct microhabitats.

Two communities of resident dolphins, Sound and Creek, were identified in
Hilton Head during my research in the 1990s. The Sound dolphins range mainly
through Calibogue Sound, which defines the west coast of Hilton Head Island,
and Broad Creek, which bisects the island, and are seen in the May and Cooper
Rivers to the west. The waters in the Sound community area are deeper and wider
than in the Creek community range; there is more boat traffic; and the area is closer
to the ocean. Dolphins in the Sound community employ distinct foraging behaviors that the transient and other resident dolphins rarely use: cooperative behaviors for corralling schools of fish and begging for food handouts from fishermen
and recreational boaters.

Dolphins in the Creek community range farther inland in shallower tidal
creeks around Bull Island and Bluffton with their exposed tidal mud flats and less
boat traffic. These dolphins employ the strand-feeding technique unique to dolphins in the coastal South Carolina and Georgia lowcountry. The Creek dolphins
also use shallow-water feeding, tail kerplunks, and pinwheeling. Since the study

area was limited, it is likely that many more communities exist in an interlocking pattern around the island and throughout the tidal sounds and creeks.

Transient dolphins tend to maintain larger groups than do resident dolphins. Several factors may account for this behavior, including different predation pressure in the ocean versus the estuaries, different prey, and foraging behaviors that might be enhanced by their greater numbers. Transient dolphins employ a unique foraging behavior not used by the resident dolphins and not reported for dolphins anywhere else in the world: they trap schools of mullet between walls of bubbles of their own creation, then take turns moving through the confused and immobilized schools, snatching fish. Along with a few resident dolphins, transients also can be seen trailing behind shrimp boats off Hilton Head Island, opportunistically feeding on fish caught in nets or thrown back by the fishermen. Transient dolphins move throughout the range of the inshore resident dolphins and are regularly observed in the coastal and ocean waters.

Social Behavior

Bottlenose dolphins interact most frequently with other community members, but they can potentially interact with a wide range of known and unknown individuals throughout their entire lives. The breadth and complexity of their behavior reflect the variety of social situations dolphins encounter, including companionship, aggression, and sexuality. Dolphin social behavior includes two dolphins slowly swimming side by side with their pectoral fins barely touching,

Sociosexual behavior has both social and sexual components. Here a male displays an erection during sociosexual behavior among several dolphins.

Sociosexual behavior is characterized by lurches, leans, bellies raised skyward, ventral-ventral swims, cartwheels, visible erections, and lots of splashing.

aggressive head butts and teeth scrapes, and sexual intercourse. Most dolphin social behaviors are subtle and difficult to interpret. Tilting and inverting the body, turning or pointing the head, blowing bubbles, and rotating or extending flippers all can be social signals. Meaning can change depending on the context, so specific movements in themselves are ambiguous.

In terms of sexual behavior, animal behaviorists distinguish between courtship and breeding since some species have elaborate courtship rituals while for some animals there is no courtship and breeding can be either lengthy or quick. Courtship (social behavior) generally functions to get animals close together for breeding (sexual behavior). For most animals, researchers can distinguish between social behavior and sexual behavior, but for dolphins, the difference is not clear-cut. Therefore, dolphin scientists consider this behavior sociosexual because there are social elements and sexual elements and often it is not possible to distinguish between the two. We cannot usually tell when actual breeding occurs in dolphins, as mating takes place underwater and can be over quickly. Even when sexual behavior is likely, most of what researchers can see is the courtship or other types of interaction. Further complicating interpretation of dolphin behavior, not all sexual interactions between dolphins are strictly procreative. For dolphins, sex often establishes and reaffirms social bonds. In fact, it has been proposed that sexual behavior is used among dolphins the way that humans use a handshake.

Social, sexual, and sociosexual behavior can be distinguished from other types of behavior (such as traveling or resting) by its direction: in all types of social behavior, actions are directed toward another dolphin. Sociosexual behavior is characterized by lurches, leans or sideways tilts, bellies raised skyward, ventral-ventral swims, cartwheels, visible erections, and lots of splashing. Sexual activity is often confused with feeding behavior when there is a lot of splashing.

Social behavior is not sociosexual behavior when there are not procreative elements. Strictly social behavior can be affiliative or aggressive. Affiliative behavior is friendly behavior that increases the connection between individuals. Simple touching and petting (for example, sliding a pectoral fin back and forth along another's side) are forms of affiliative behavior. Spy hops (poking the head straight up out of the water), nudges, body rubs, tail slaps, and breaches, in which the dolphin launches itself vertically out of the water and lands on its side or belly with a loud crash, are also commonly seen when dolphins are interacting positively.

There is bound to be occasional conflict among social animals, and dolphins are no exception. Aggressive behavior arising from conflicts between two or more individuals can escalate to raking (scraping one's teeth along the skin of another), biting, tail swatting, and ramming. Aggressive attacks are preceded by a series of graded warnings, exaggerated movements that increase the dolphin's apparent size and are meant to intimidate the opponent to avoid a fight. The mildest warning

Spy hops, nudges, body rubs, tail slaps, and breaches are commonly seen during affiliative interactions. Here, an adult male spy hops to get a better view of the water's surface around him.

Dolphins interact with a wide variety of animals in myriad ways. Here, a dolphin teases a pelican, chasing and jumping over it.

signals are the release of a burst of air as a large bubble and an open-mouth display of teeth. Jaw snapping and sharp head and tail jerks follow. The extreme warning signal is the *s* posture in which the dolphin lowers its head and tail and arches its back.

Travel and play are two kinds of behavior that can be but are not necessarily social. Both can be accomplished alone, with no social component, but both also can be conducted in the company of other dolphins, adding a social component. Dolphins often have an intimate knowledge of the area they inhabit and purposely move from one place to another. Forward movement is a component of nearly every dolphin behavior, so dolphin researchers define travel specifically. Travel is moving directly from point A to point B. It is characterized in dolphins by regular, rhythmic breathing patterns and movement in a straight line. Often dolphins will leap, porpoise (surface quickly to breathe several times in a row), or use an undulating swim, surfacing and submerging rhythmically, while traveling. Generally little interaction occurs among group members as they travel. There are various intensities of travel—the tempo may be fast or slow, and the most common is somewhere between the extremes.

In the scientific world, play is defined as non–goal-oriented behavior: the dolphins are doing what appears to be fun and for no other reason than it is fun.

There are no definite behavioral components used to identify play. In terrestrial animals, we can nearly always recognize play because we are familiar with the animals' postures and facial expressions. Usually, the behaviors are similar to those found in other contexts such as fighting but with body movements so exaggerated that it is obviously play. Dolphin play can be recognized in the same way. Dolphins often bowride for fun or play with strands of grass, bird feathers, or other inanimate objects either alone or with another dolphin. Some even play with other animals, including fish and birds.

Another aspect of dolphin behavior that is not well understood is sleep. Research on captive dolphins has revealed that dolphins spend about thirty-three percent of the day sleeping—about the same amount as humans.

The way that dolphins sleep has perplexed scientists for decades. Sleep is problematic for dolphins because they live in the water and must breathe air regularly. They cannot curl up in a cave, protected from predators. Because they are conscious breathers thinking about each breath and the actions necessary to accomplish each breath, dolphins cannot completely lose awareness as humans do when sleeping. Researchers believe that dolphins rest their brains while remaining somewhat conscious of the world around them. Since dolphins are not fully unconscious when they sleep, dolphin researchers generally refer to dolphins as "resting" rather than sleeping.

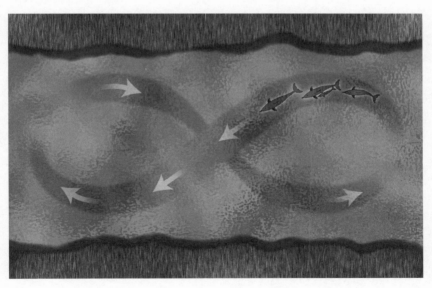

Hilton Head dolphins sometimes rest while moving together in a stereotypical figure-eight pattern. Resting in this manner can last several hours. The figure-eight pattern allows dolphins to be aware of their surroundings in all directions.

A dolphin rests in a horizontal position that does not change, even as the dolphin rises to the water surface to breathe.

Dolphin rest is characterized by slow, deep breathing, and it usually includes vertical movement as the dolphin sinks underwater to rest and rises to the surface again to breathe. Dolphins in aquariums will sometimes rest with one eye closed and one open, an indicator of the dolphin's presumed ability to rest one side of its brain at a time. The unique structure of the dolphin's brain makes this independent function possible, as the hemispheres of its brain (unlike those of humans) are not connected, thus allowing each half to function independently of the other. Each eye connects only to one side, the opposite side of the brain—the right eye transmits information to the left brain and vice versa—making it likely that the dolphin rests one half of its brain at a time.

In my 1994–1998 research, three distinct resting behaviors were observed in the Hilton Head area. Groups of dolphins sometimes rest together while moving slowly in a circle or a figure eight. This behavior can last several hours and is often observed during the day. Dolphins also rest while remaining in one place, either on the surface or underwater. When surface resting, dolphins float at the surface with only part of their melon (top of their head) above the water. The rest of their body hangs almost straight down below the head. When resting underwater, the dolphins maintain a horizontal orientation and regularly surface with their entire back exposed; they sink straight down again after taking a breath of air.

From a functional point of view, dolphin rest is a cessation of activity. Rest is commonly seen in quiet waterways rather than busy channels, so researchers or boaters rarely observe it. Resting dolphins will stay fairly close to each other (within one body length), positioned side by side or in a circle.

Rest is recognized by the even tempo of slow surfacing behavior and slow inhalations and exhalations. There is no interaction among individual dolphins, and any forward movement is slow and limited. Hilton Head dolphins do not exhibit diurnal patterns; their environment changes more with the movement of the tides. Since their behavior is tied to the cycles of the tides, they can be active or resting at any time of the day or night.

CHAPTER THREE

DOLPHIN CONSERVATION

The east coast bottlenose dolphin population is still recovering from a massive and unprecedented die-off that began in 1987. Between June 1987 and March 1988, hundreds of dead bottlenose dolphins washed ashore from New Jersey to Florida. The first carcass was found in New Jersey and the last on Florida's east coast eleven months later. Seven hundred and forty dead dolphins were counted, but the exact toll is unknown; it is highly likely that a large number of dolphins were not recovered. This loss represents an estimated half of the entire migrating stock, which was subsequently classified as "depleted" by the United States government under the Endangered Species Act. Resident dolphins, inhabiting in-shore bays and estuaries, appeared unaffected; all but one stranding occurred on outer coastal beaches, and no known animals from inshore locales, such as the Indian or Banana Rivers in Florida, were found with clinical signs of the epidemic.

Early pathological findings suggested that brevetoxin, a neurotoxin produced by the dinoflagellate *Ptychodiscus brevis* in a red-tide event, was the proximate cause of the mass mortality. However, only 47 percent of the examined animals

Dolphins approach a boat and open their mouths to beg for food from people in the boat. Feeding wild dolphins has been illegal in the United States since 1990.

Feeding dolphins can be dangerous to both humans and dolphins. Dolphins have been known to bite and ram humans, causing serious injuries and the death of one man in Brazil. Eating inappropriate foods can lead to illness and disease for dolphins.

tested positive for the toxin. Further, most necropsies (animal autopsies) indicated that animals had a variety of chronic disorders and secondary infections associated with immune suppression and therefore did not die directly from the brevetoxin. Researchers now suggest that sublethal exposure to brevetoxin adversely affected the health of exposed animals through a variety of mechanisms, leaving them more vulnerable to ubiquitous opportunistic pathogens. After several years of research, the die-off also was shown to be associated with morbillivirus, a naturally occurring distemper virus related to the virus that causes measles in humans.

These results suggest that the dolphins resident in the inland waterways were somehow protected from or unexposed to the lethal agents that killed migratory individuals. This pattern of strandings and the disease progression reveal that two or more distinct groups or "stocks" of dolphins existed within the population. In 1997 the National Marine Fisheries Service established a multiple-method program to identify the stock structure of bottlenose dolphins along the U.S. Atlantic coast. Currently, it is assumed that coastal dolphins from New Jersey to Florida form two stocks, one residential and one migratory. However, ongoing research casts doubt on this assumption; it currently appears that there are most likely many stocks of dolphins, each representing a distinct and unique community with its own ranging, foraging, breeding, and association patterns.

Each community faces differing conservation pressures depending upon its ranging and foraging patterns. For instance, dolphins in northern North Carolina face intense pressure from a variety of commercial and recreational fisheries, and nearly half of the stranded dolphins examined show clear signs of human-induced mortality, either directly through violence or indirectly by becoming entangled in fishing lines and nets. These fisheries do not operate in South Carolina, so dolphins living here are not affected by them.

Hilton Head dolphins face other threats to their health and their lives. Probably the most serious threat is handouts of food. Many local dolphins will approach boats, check out the humans in them, and beg for food.

But humans should not feed these dolphins. There are several reasons not to promote this particular interspecies interaction. Feeding wild animals substantially alters their natural behavior. Provisioned Hilton Head dolphins (those fed by boaters) spend more time alone and in smaller groups, and this may make the dolphins more vulnerable to shark attacks. Handouts make it harder for dolphins to find their own food and for juveniles to learn hunting skills from adults. Also, provisioned dolphins that beg at boats are more aggressive with each other, often hitting or ramming each other in an attempt to get free food. This aggression can even lead to death.

Dolphins approach a crab fisherman's boat, opening their mouths to beg for fish taken from the raised metal wire crab trap. Fish are regularly replaced as the caught crabs are harvested.

PHOTO BY THOMAS MURPHY

Dolphins are exposed to natural predators, pathogens, and diseases. This adult male dolphin, dubbed Choppy, bears the scars of an encounter with a predatory shark.

Provisioned dolphins will eventually lose their natural wariness of humans, leaving them open to injury or even death, a risk illustrated by the scars many dolphins have received from boat propellers. People, including fishermen, have been known to shoot dolphins for sport or to protect the fishermen's gear or catch. One dolphin died in Hilton Head in 1994 after an unprovoked attack by a boater, a tragedy that might not have happened if the dolphin had not lost its natural caution.

Dolphins often get caught in fishing lines and occasionally get tangled in the lines on crab pots. This dolphin has a permanent reminder of an encounter with a rope.

Because dolphins have no sense of smell, and are grasp-and-swallow feeders, they cannot discriminate between good food and bad food. Many Hilton Head dolphins eat just about anything offered to them, even though most of it will make them sick later. Dolphins are designed to catch and eat healthy, live fish, not dead fish, sandwiches, or potato chips. In 1993, one dolphin in Florida was fed spoiled fish contaminated with bacteria that caused the dolphin's brain to swell; it subsequently died a slow, painful death, swimming erratically in tight circles, beating its head against a barnacle-encrusted pier, and finally beaching itself on land.

Feeding dolphins is also dangerous to humans—dolphins can and do bite the hand that feeds them when more food is not quickly forthcoming. Several people have gone to the emergency room after discovering the muscular force behind the dolphin smile and the piercing ability of those pointy teeth. Additionally, diseases can be transmitted between dolphins and humans and vice versa.

Finally, it is illegal to feed dolphins. A 1996 amendment to the Marine Mammal Protection Act prohibits feeding or swimming with any marine mammal in U.S. waters. Feeding is considered harassment under this law, and hefty fines are levied on those caught interfering with normal dolphin activity.

Hilton Head dolphins are easily seen at close range without being fed. Dolphins in their natural state are an important part of the local ecosystem—a critical

In addition to natural threats, Hilton Head dolphins must navigate around boats and ships. Many dolphins have been hit by boats, as illustrated by this calf's missing dorsal fin, which was severed by a boat propeller.

piece of nature's puzzle whose loss leads to ecosystem imbalance. Careless attempts to interact with dolphins can negatively impact these creatures we admire so much. We can best show our admiration by respecting their need to lead natural lives undisturbed by humans. The local dolphins present ample opportunities for inter-species interaction and education, seemingly unperturbed by slow-moving boats, thus allowing boaters close observation.

Historically, however, contact between humans and dolphins has been harm-ful to the dolphins. In the recent past, bottlenose dolphins were hunted for meat, leather, oil, and meal for fertilizer and animal feed. In some parts of the world, many species of dolphins still are hunted for food and bait. Until 1928, a dolphin fishery operated off beaches in North Carolina.

Although dolphins are no longer hunted for food in this country, the fate of dolphins is still tied to our actions. Marine pollution severely threatens dolphin health. Ingested human-generated debris can choke dolphins or block their diges-tion, resulting in slow starvation. Industrial and domestic waste also is degrading dolphin habitats. And runoff from storm drains brings toxins into local water-ways. Dolphins feed at the top of the food chain and accumulate toxins in their body tissues over the course of their lives. Through consumption of human-produced contaminants such as polychlorinated biphenyls (PCBs) and organochlorides, dol-phin immune systems may become overstressed and less able to fight off natural

invaders. Female dolphins live longer than males, giving them more time to accumulate toxins in their bodies, many of which are stored in body fat. Females
dump their toxin load to their calves by metabolizing fat to produce milk. Often
females will lose their first-born calf because of this input of toxins.

Dolphins also are exposed to natural predators, pathogens, and diseases. They
can suffer from viral, bacterial, and fungal infections; stomach ulcers; skin
diseases; tumors; heart disease; urogenital disorders; and respiratory disorders.
Some large shark species, including tiger, dusky, and bull sharks, are predators of
bottlenose dolphins. Parasites that typically affect dolphins include tapeworms,
flukes, and roundworms. Many local dolphins carry a heavy load of lung and
other parasites and battle heart disease and opportunistic viruses.

Our shared coastal environment is finite. Dolphin habitats are decreasing with
our steady encroachment into their fragile environment, especially in the marsh
nurseries where their prey mature.

The fact that we share the top of the marine food web with dolphins inevitably
leads to interactions between dolphins and human fisheries. Many dolphins are
injured and killed along the east coast each year. Gill nets, drift nets, and purse
seines are the main threats. Dolphins also can get caught in fishing lines and occasionally become tangled in the lines on crab pots. Dolphins also must contend
with local boats and ships; many dolphins in Hilton Head waterways carry scars
from collisions with boats, particularly boat propellers, which will slice the dolphin's
dorsal fin, either cutting it off or permanently damaging it.

*Adult dolphins are vulnerable to damage from collisions with boats. This dolphin's fin
was cut several times by a boat propeller.*

Boats and jet skis approaching dolphins too quickly, too unpredictably, or too closely cause dolphins stress. Chasing dolphins decreases their energy reserves necessary to survive in a harsh environment. Boats and jet skis have accidentally hit dolphins. Boat disturbance can lower calf survival rates by disrupting nursing and resting behaviors. Disturbing dolphins causes them varying degrees of stress, depending on how traumatic the incident, and stress alters feeding behavior and increases energy expenditure. Such stress decreases the general health of dolphins and increases the risk of contracting diseases through a lowered immune response. Swimming with or riding on dolphins can be life threatening for them through this stress response.

Dolphin conservation is not selfless; as we protect dolphins and their environment, we are also protecting ourselves, our environment, and our natural resources. As coastal residents and visitors, it is in our interest to monitor the waters for pollutants and minimize marine pollution. As boaters, we must navigate carefully around dolphins to avoid collisions and prevent disturbances to natural behaviors. We have a long history together, and with care and thought we can maintain a positive relationship.

COMMONLY ASKED QUESTIONS

What is the difference between dolphins and porpoises?

Both dolphins and porpoises are odontocetes—toothed whales. The terms formerly were used interchangeably to denote any medium-sized odontocete, but scientists now use the terms more specifically. Dolphins are odontocetes belonging to the scientific family Delphinidae, while porpoises belong to the family Phocoenidae. Physical differences distinguish dolphins and porpoises: dolphins are larger (averaging eight feet long) than porpoises (averaging five feet long), and dolphins have conical teeth while porpoises have spade-shaped teeth.

Are dolphins fish?

Although they live in the water, dolphins are not fish but are mammals. Like all mammals, they breathe air, bear live young who they suckle with milk that the mothers produce, and have hair at some point in their lives.

How often do dolphins have to breathe? How long can they hold their breath?

Dolphins generally take two to three breaths per minute, but they can hold their breath for up to ten minutes. It takes them about a third of a second to exchange nearly 90 percent of the air in their lungs during each breath.

How fast can dolphins swim?

Dolphins routinely swim at speeds of three to seven miles per hour, but they can achieve burst speeds of eighteen to twenty-two miles per hour for short periods of time.

How long do dolphins live?

Dolphins can live up to fifty years in the wild but more commonly live only into their twenties.

How do dolphins sleep?

Dolphins sleep by resting (or turning off) one hemisphere of their brains at a time, swimming slowly, or remaining stationary at or below the water's surface. Like humans, dolphins spend about a third of the day sleeping.

Do dolphins really have midwives and aunts?

When a dolphin mother gives birth, she may have one or more dolphins with her. These dolphins do not actually participate in the birth but are there when it occurs. Adult or juvenile females that are associates of a mother may act as "aunts," watching the baby dolphin as its mother forages or interacts with other dolphins.

DOLPHINS: MYTH AND REALITY

Racing alongside a boat or leaping in front of the setting sun, dolphins have been capturing human hearts for centuries. Dolphins are featured prominently in the mythology, art, and folklore of many ancient peoples. For example, ancient Maori believed dolphins to be messengers of the gods, and pre-Hellenic Greeks worshiped dolphins as gods in themselves. Modern myths attest to the dolphins' enduring ability to ignite our imagination, but these myths often obscure the truth.

Dolphins are subject to myth making from the moment they are born. For example, many people believe that a dolphin must push its newborn to the surface for its first breath. In reality, the dolphin baby is able to swim on its own to the surface. Often, a mother will nudge the baby to guide it in a certain direction. This action may look like the infant is being pushed, but usually the baby is swimming and breathing on its own at the surface before the mother even reaches its side.

Another common misconception is that dolphins need midwives to help with the birth. According to modern legend, these "aunts" actually help pull the infant out as it is born or even push it to the surface for its first breath. Although other dolphins may be present at a birth, none assist with the birth. When the infant is older, adult or adolescent companions may babysit the infant while the mother feeds. Sometimes even what looks like babysitting might actually be teenagers "stealing" the baby for a while in order to practice mothering skills, according to researchers in Australia.

The most prevalent myth about dolphins is that because they always appear to be smiling, they are always happy. This permanent grin, however, is an effect of their not having cheeks. Dolphins are grasp-and-swallow feeders, so they do not need cheeks, which are useful only if food is chewed before being swallowed. The muscles at the jaw determine how their face looks and do not reflect their disposition.

The always-happy myth has spawned two related myths. The first is that dolphins are always altruistic and helpful. Sadly, this is not the case. In the fall of 1994, I spent three days observing an injured dolphin as part of an attempt to rehabilitate it. This dolphin was unable to eat on its own and was deteriorating to the point that by the third day, it was difficult for it to find the energy to surface and breathe on its own. Although the injured dolphin encountered many other dolphins during this time, not one assisted it or even paid any attention to it. The second related myth is that dolphins are always gentle, never aggressive. Although the image of such gentle creatures is a pleasant one, it is unrealistic. Many dolphins fight and will rake each other with their sharp teeth if threats and warnings do not work. These rakes leave parallel lines of scars on the skin of the victim, appearing much like a fork was scraped down its back or head. Males also kidnap and herd females aggressively in order to mate with them. In fact, many males will gang up on a female and hold her captive for hours, days, or even weeks.

After fighting, dolphins usually will make up with each other. The prevalent belief that dolphins have a complex social structure similar to ours is true. The ability to fight and make up is one indicator of this complexity. Dolphins have strong family bonds, pair bonds, and relationships similar to the ones we have with close friends, acquaintances, and family. They also form coalitions—groupings for specific purposes that change based on the activity at hand—another hallmark of complex social structure. In fact, dolphin societies are probably more complex than currently realized. Research continues to provide facts about dolphins that are often more unlikely than the myths we have created.

GLOSSARY

acoustic   pertaining to the sense of hearing or sound.

adult   a socially and sexually mature animal, fully grown and able to reproduce.

aquatic   living or growing in fresh or salt water.

blubber   the layer of fat below the skin of marine mammals used to insulate the body. This layer replaced the fur of terrestrial mammals through evolution.

breach   a leap completely or partially out of the water, generally ending with the whale or dolphin landing on its side or back.

calf   a young dolphin still dependent upon its mother, usually from birth through three or four years.

cetacea   order of the class Mammalia that includes whales, dolphins, and porpoises.

dolphin   a marine mammal of the family Delphinidae. Dolphins are found in all oceans of the world and in some fresh water rivers. A dolphin is cylindrical in shape with an elongated beak, conical teeth, two pectoral fins, a dorsal fin, and flukes. The terms dolphin and porpoise were formerly used interchangeably, but the two families are now distinguished from each other.

dorsal   the upper part of a dolphin; the back of a dolphin.

dorsal fin   fin on a dolphin's back that is believed to be important for steering and balance.

echolocation   the sensory system of toothed whales, bats, and dolphins in which the animal emits high frequency sounds and orients itself based on the reflected sound waves. Echolocation is generally associated with foraging and traveling behavior but also might have tactile and social functions.

evolution   the scientific theory that groups of organisms (for example, populations or species) change over time due to external forces acting to promote the reproduction of the most fit individuals. This change results in descendant populations exhibiting physiological, anatomical, and behavioral differences from their ancestors.

flukes   the horizontal tail of the dolphin or whale used for propulsion through the water.

habituated   accustomed to close human presence or feeding through long exposure; fed by humans.

juvenile   a sexually and socially immature animal that has not yet reproduced or reached its full size.

mammal   any of a group of vertebrate animals, including dolphins and humans, that have a notochord, have hair at some point in their lives, give birth, and feed the young milk from the mother's mammary glands.

marine   living or growing in salt water.

melon   the fatty bulb of flesh on a dolphin's forehead.

migration   the movement of an animal species or population from one place to another.

mysticete   any of the several species of large whales with baleen instead of teeth.

neonate   a newborn animal. Dolphins are generally considered neonates for three months. Neonates can be recognized by their dark skin, lighter vertical fetal folds, and clumsy breathing behavior.

odontocete   any of the several species of whales, dolphins, and porpoises with teeth.

pod   a large group of interacting and potentially related whales or dolphins.

porpoise   a member of the scientific family Phocoenidae. There are six
                  recognized porpoise species. These generally have blunt heads
                  and flat, spade-shaped teeth. The terms dolphin and porpoise
                  used to be used interchangeably, but the two families are now
                  distinguished from each other.

provisioned   fed by humans.

rostrum   the elongated beak (or mouth) of a dolphin.

terrestrial   living or growing on land.

ventral   the underside of the dolphin, including the chest and belly.

whale   generally, can be any member of the order Cetacea.
                  Specifically, any of the several species of baleen or large,
                  toothed whales.

BIBLIOGRAPHY

General Books

May, J. 1990. *The Greenpeace Book of Dolphins* (New York: Sterling Publishing Company).

Norris, K. 1974. *The Porpoise Watcher* (New York: W. W. Norton and Company).

————. 1991. *Dolphin Days: The Life and Times of the Spinner Dolphin* (New York: W. W. Norton and Company).

Pryor, K. 1975. *Lads before the Wind* (North Bend, Ind.: Sunshine Books).

Ridgway, S. 1987. *The Dolphin Doctor* (New York: Fawcett Crest).

Shane, S. 1988. *The Bottlenose Dolphin in the Wild* (San Carlos, Calif.: Hatcher Trade Press).

Thompson, P., and B. Wilson. 1994. *Bottlenose Dolphins* (Stillwater, Okla.: Voyageur Press).

Scientific Books

Alcock, J. 1989. *Animal Behavior,* 4th edition. (Sunderland, Mass.: Sinauer Associates, Inc.).

Gaskin, D. E. 1982. *The Ecology of Whales and Dolphins* (Portsmouth, N.H.: Heinemann Educational Books).

Herman, L. 1980. *Cetacean Behavior: Mechanisms and Functions* (New York: John Wiley and Sons).

Leatherwood, S., and R. Reeves. 1983. *Sierra Club Handbook of Whales and Dolphins* (San Francisco: Sierra Club Books).

————, eds. *The Bottlenose Dolphin* (San Diego: Academic Press, 1990).

Mann, J. et al., eds. 2000. *Cetacean Societies: Field Studies of Whales and Dolphins* (Chicago: University of Chicago Press).

Pryor, K., and K. Norris. 1991. *Dolphin Societies: Discoveries and Puzzles* (Berkeley and Los Angeles: University of California Press).

Reynolds, J. III, and S. Rommel, eds. 1999. *Biology of Marine Mammals* (Washington, D.C.: Smithsonian Institution Press).

Reynolds, J. III, R. Wells, and S. Eide. 2000. *The Bottlenose Dolphin: Biology and Conservation* (Gainesville: University Press of Florida).

Tweiss, J. Jr., and R. Reeves, eds. 1999. *Conservation and Management of Marine Mammals* (Washington, D.C.: Smithsonian Institution Press).

Books for Young Readers

Adamson, D. 2000. *Stormy the Baby Dolphin: A Gulf Coast Rescue* (Austin, Tex.: Eakin Press).

Behrens, J. 1990. *Dolphins!* (Chicago: Children's Press).

Bridge, L. 1976. *The Playful Dolphins* (Washington, D.C.: National Geographic Society).

Brust, B. 1990. *Zoobooks: Dolphins and Porpoises* (San Diego, Calif.: Wildlife Education Ltd.).

Field, Nancy, and Sally Machlis. 1989. *Discovering Marine Mammals: A Learning and Activity Book.* 3d printing (Corvallis, Oreg.: Dog-Eared Publications).

Gay, T. 1991. *Whales and Dolphins in Action* (New York: Aladdin Books).

George, T. 1996. *A Dolphin Named Bob* (New York: Harper Collins Publishers).

Gibbons, G. 1991. *Whales* (New York: Holiday House).

Hatherly, J., and D. Nicholls. 1990. *Dolphins and Porpoises* (New York: Facts on File).

Jacobs, F. 1977. *Sounds in the Sea* (New York: William Morrow and Co.).

Kovacs, D. 1994. *All About Dolphins!* (Bridgeport, Conn.: Third Story Books).

Lauber, P. 1995. *The Friendly Dolphins* (New York: Scholastic).

Morris, R. 1975. *Dolphin* (New York: Harper and Row).

O'Dell, S. 1960. *Island of the Blue Dolphins* (Boston: Houghton Mifflin Company).

Orr, K. 1995. *Story of a Dolphin* (Minneapolis, Minn.: Carolrhoda Books).

Overbeck, C. 1976. *Splash, the Dolphin* (Minneapolis, Minn.: Carolrhoda Books).

Reeves, R., and S. 1987. Leatherwood. *The Sea World Book of Dolphins* (San Diego, Calif.: Harcourt Brace Jovanovich).

Stonehouse, B. 1978. *A Closer Look at Whales and Dolphins* (New York: Gloucester Press).

Websites

American Cetacean Society. **www.acsonline.org**

Cetacean Society International. **http://elfi.com/csihome**

International Whaling Commission. **http://ourworld.compuserve.com/home-pages/iwcoffice**

National Aquarium, Baltimore. **www.aqua.com**

Sea World, Inc. **www.seaworld.com**

Society for Marine Mammalogy. **http://pegasus.cc.ucf.edu/smm/**

United Kingdom Cetacean Network. **www.egroups.com/group/UKCetnet**

Whalenet. **http://whale.wheelock.edu**

INDEX